GOD LOVES
YOU WITH AN
EVERLASTING
LOVE

God Loves You with an Everlasting Love
Copyright @ 2004, 2012, Patricia King

Published by XP Publishing
P. O. Box 1017
Maricopa, Arizona 85139
XPpublishing.com

ISBN: 978-1-936101-83-2

GOD LOVES
YOU WITH AN
EVERLASTING
LOVE

PATRICIA KING

TABLE OF CONTENTS

From the desk of Patricia King...

Dear Reader,

There is nothing better in life than knowing beyond a doubt that you are unconditionally and perfectly loved! Countless individuals spend their entire lives attempting to satisfy the cries of the empty and lonely places within – the places that long for the comfort and security that only love can fill.

Where does one find such love and satisfaction? Can you really experience this kind of security and well-being? Is it actually possible to know the value and preciousness of who you were created to be?

This short book is designed to introduce you to the greatest revelation anyone could ever receive. It is the revelation of God's unconditional love for you – the love that was perfectly tested and proven at the Cross, 2000 years ago.

There is no one like you. You were created as an object of His affection, acceptance and love, and it was never God's desire for you to experience rejection or abandonment. You were made to be a recipient of His bountiful grace and favor.

May you drink deeply of this revelation and come to a full realization that:

God loves you with an everlasting love!

Patricia King

1

The God Kind of Love

"Behold what *manner* of love the Father has bestowed on us, *that we should be called children of God*" (1 John 3:1 NKJV, emphasis mine).

What manner of love would motivate a perfect, holy, and righteous God to offer a sinful and rebellious person the right to become His very own dear child and heir of all that He is and all that He has? It sounds like an extravagant act, doesn't it? This, however, is indeed the very manner of love the Father has shown to each and every one of us. Nothing throughout all the history of mankind has ever been able to make Him withdraw this love, although we have all put His love to the test over and over again. The demonstration of this love is unchangeable because He is unchangeable.

Many individuals regularly waver in their assurance of God's love and continually question their right standing with Him. The lack of this assurance breeds insecurity. They might ask, "Am I worthy enough? Do I love God enough? Am I performing well enough? Am I serving Him enough?"

My faith constantly wavered just like this before I understood the clear revelation of Christ's work on the Cross that demonstrated His eternal, unchangeable love for me. During those years, I always questioned my value in His sight. This produced striving, tension and unrest. Without the assurance of His unchanging love, you are never free to be. If you are not free to be, you will never be free to do. It is the revelation of His love that produces fullness, freedom, and fruitfulness in life.

First John 4:16-19 teaches us that, *"There is no fear in love ... We love, because He first loved us."* When you understand the unconditional love of God, the fear of not being accepted and loved by Him is eliminated. You know deep within that you're His precious one and you're assured of your place in His heart forever. When you have this type of assurance, even when everything in your life is unsettled, you feel secure. Love gives you an unshakeable confidence that He will work everything out and keep you in perfect peace.

Romans 8:32-39 informs us that the love the Father has given us is greater than any other force. It confidently assures us that nothing can separate us from His love. In fact, you can never be separated from the love of God that is in Christ Jesus – NEVER. In Christ, you are forever sealed in His holy love. Oh, how wonderful!

You probably weren't loved unconditionally in your childhood (just as others weren't) so from time to time lying thoughts might have assaulted your mind: I'm not loveable. I'm not accepted. I haven't been able to accomplish enough. I have no value. I can't succeed.

The Word, however, says that you are perfectly loved and nothing at all can ever separate you from it. When you really start to understand this truth, you will be able to cast down the tormenting lies of rejection, inferiority, and insecurity. The power of God's love and favor will prevail, causing the lies to fall. Then you will experience what you were created to be from the foundation of the world – an object of His deep love and affection.

God wants you to feel so secure in His love that you will be able to go anywhere, do anything, face any spirit of rejection, and overcome any obstacle. You will be able to say with confidence, "I am a precious, loved child of God. I am His favored one."

Love is God's mark on our lives. Not only are we to know His love for ourselves, but we are to extravagantly share it with others. Once you know you are a loved one, His love in you will spill out all over the place and touch others – you won't be able to help it! This type of love doesn't come from an inward striving to be a loving person. It comes from knowing who you are as a perfectly loved child. Then His powerful grace flows through you like a river and offers refreshing to those around you.

A PERSONAL TESTIMONY

I remember so clearly what life was like without Christ and the revelation of His love. I was a young career woman, a wife, and mother of two boys, yet totally unfulfilled and broken. Most of my brokenness, however, was hidden to the onlooker. I wore an invisible mask of well-being because I was afraid to let people see the real me. What if they rejected me? How could I ever cope with that? I constantly lived behind the many disguises that concealed the guilt and shame that plagued my heart regularly. I was in an invisible prison and I couldn't escape.

I tried everything to become free. I attended numerous self-help courses and joined new age/occult enlightenment groups, hoping to find some answers for my distressed soul. I regularly imbibed in a variety of addictive substances in an effort to find comfort and relief. I also attempted to find meaning for life through work, career, and taking extra college courses. Every effort failed terribly to offer any liberty. I became increasingly unstable emotionally, with no way to get a grip on things. The more I tried, the more I failed. The more I failed, the more discouraged and bound I became. The tentacles of fear, shame and guilt wrapped themselves around me, continuously strangling any tinge of hope. I was constantly plagued with a sense of powerlessness in life.

I was a mess and totally out of control! I desperately needed help but didn't know where to turn. God hears the cries of our heart and He definitely heard mine. It was following a near-death experience, at the lowest point of my life, that the Lord sent a wonderful man to share the gospel with me. He was an Anglican minister named Reverend Ron Hunt. I will never forget the first evening I attended the little home Bible study at his invitation. Although I was nervous to step into that unfamiliar environment, I was pleasantly surprised as I witnessed a sincere group of people who obviously knew God in a very personal way. One after another that evening, they shared testimonies of how Jesus had changed their lives. They claimed that He forgave their sins, cleansed them from guilt and shame, and offered them a brand new life. Wow! That was exactly what I wanted... but was it possible?

Following the meeting I went home and, while alone kneeling on my living room floor, I cried out to this unseen God for help. "Jesus, I have nothing to offer You except my brokenness. I have made a big mess of my life, but I would really like You to come into my heart and make me new – just like You did for those people up the street." I honestly did not know if Jesus would want to come into my life or not. I felt so evil and had no confidence that He would be able to love the likes of me. Yet to my amazement, He didn't hesitate to enter my heart. I hadn't even finished praying when I literally felt the presence of liquid love come into my being. The One who knew every wicked detail of my life didn't hesitate for a moment to show me His extravagant mercy and acceptance. I literally felt the pressure of my sin leave me, along with all the guilt and shame. It was as though a prison door had been opened and I was allowed to run free. I felt lovely and beautiful inside for the very first time I could remember.

All I could do was cry. In fact, I cried all night while I worshipped Him. No one had to teach me to worship – when you are deeply touched by His love, worship is just a normal response... it is the only response! Everything in you is so thankful, so grateful. I knew beyond a shadow of a doubt that this gift of love had nothing to do with my own ability to fix myself. I had already proven through constant failed attempts that I was "unfixable." This gift had nothing to do with me. This was a free gift of life – His gift of everlasting, unbendable, unchangeable, unshakable and unfailing love! Yeah, God!

The next number of years were extremely fulfilling for me as I daily experienced increased revelation of His Word and His ways. His love healed, delivered and established me in a brand new life. It had nothing at all to do with my efforts. This new life was His gift. It is a gift that can't be earned and it is available to everyone. It is available to you!

I began to serve the Lord with passion. I never for a moment felt a pressure to serve Him – I served Him because I loved Him. It's what you do when you're in love. My entire life changed. I had new friends, new interests and new desires. I wanted to spend my entire life serving the One who had loved me so perfectly. Year after year was filled with a continual unfolding of His goodness.

In my experience as a young Christian, I had never tasted "legalism" (legalism is an attempt to secure right standing with the Lord through obedience to the Law). I was first introduced to this type of religious bondage when our family served the Lord on a foreign mission field (my husband began following Jesus a year after me). The leaders of the mission center were very passionate for the Lord and I know they meant well. Unfortunately, they did not understand that the Lord's unconditional love is a gift and cannot be earned through our works. As a result, they taught those they worked with to perfect themselves through self-effort in order to please God. The leaders themselves also lived under this same burden. I experienced a daily performance pressure on this mission field.

In all my striving to do well, I constantly believed I was falling short of what was expected. I was convinced I was disappointing God, and the more I tried to please Him the more I failed. The more I failed the more I strove within. The cycle continued with increasing despair. This type of pressure was bringing me right back into the torment and bondage I experienced prior to knowing Christ. I was plagued with the same guilt and the same shame. It simply showed up wearing different clothes. One was a cloak of unrighteousness and the other was one of self-righteousness. Both were deadly and bore the same fruit of devastation.

After serving on this mission field as faithfully and diligently as I could for over six months, I finished our term feeling spiritually bankrupt. I had even lost assurance of my salvation. I believed I had totally failed the Lord and that He would never have any use for me again. I believed that I was no longer a precious child to Him – I had disappointed Him too deeply. What a deception I had stepped into!

On my return home from this mission experience, some friends helped me to rightly divide the Word and to trust that the Lord still loved me. The healing and restoration did not come overnight. At times, I was still plagued with the fear of being rejected by God and I constantly battled self-condemnation. I cried out constantly for relief. All I wanted was to feel close to God – to feel worthy of His love and to know I was pleasing Him.

It was years later that I finally received a revelation of the Cross. This revelation delivered me from the torment and fear that had bound my soul, and became an anchor for my faith forever. The revelation of the Cross and the covenant Christ made with God on our behalf is

an absolute foundation for understanding His unconditional love. The day I received this revelation, I wept for
hours on end, completely in awe of His loving-kindness
– completely amazed at His grace.

It is one thing to be touched by the love of God and
enjoy the experience of it, like I had as a young Christian.
It is another thing, however, to be fully anchored in the
unshakable, unfailing revelation of the doctrine of His
unconditional love. Jesus said, "You will know the truth,
and the truth will make you free" (John 8:32). The day
the revelation of the doctrine of the Cross filled my heart
was the day I knew I would walk free forever. Regardless
of what circumstances surrounded my life, regardless of
how many condemning thoughts my mind received, I
now had an eternal place to stand. I was anchored forever in His love because I understood the truth of it! I
am blood-bought into an eternal love covenant that can
never be broken. What freedom this truth brings!

In this writing, I am committed to introducing you
to this life-changing, life-sustaining doctrine. May you
come to know the revelation of this truth so deeply
within your heart that your entire being will forever be
filled and anchored in it. I desire you to walk through the
following pages with expectation and focus as the Holy
Spirit unfolds the most profound and life-altering doctrine in the entire Bible – the Cross and the Covenant.
This doctrine reveals God's true heart of unfailing, tested
love. He loves you with an everlasting love. He really
does. You will see!

2

GOD CHOSE YOU!

God wanted you! You weren't a mistake, regardless of the circumstances that surrounded your birth. Perhaps you weren't planned by your parents or maybe your conception was the result of an unfortunate incident. Even in cases as sad as these, you need to know that God had you in His heart from before the foundation of the world. He planned you. His ultimate desire was for you to be conceived and brought forth in a beautiful, pure atmosphere of parental love and affection. Tragically, everyone has fallen short of His perfect ways because of our sinful, imperfect nature. God planned for you to come forth into the realm of time and fulfill His eternal purpose for your life. His potential in you is fun to explore.

God actually wanted to have a family. That's why most folks desire to have children; that desire comes from Him. Mankind has been created in His likeness and therefore, when you find yourself longing to have children you are simply identifying with His passion. He wanted children and that's why you do, too (unless you've been emotionally wounded or have a special call to remain single).

In the beginning, God created trees, flowers, birds, fish, animals and a host of other earthly and celestial things. He loved everything He created and each day He said, "It is good." Even though He was very pleased, He still longed for a precious creation made in His likeness – an object of His affection to fulfill the longing of His righteous heart. My husband, Ron, and I did not have children in our first year of marriage. We did however have pets – two dogs.

Although we enjoyed our dogs and they were like family, they did not satisfy our longing for children. The dogs were nice, but not *that* nice. There was something inside us that said, "Children, children, children." That longing was a small taste of what the Lord felt in His heart for us. The dogs and other creatures were not enough for Him, either. Although He took pleasure in them, they did not satisfy His desire to have YOU! Passionate desire for you was burning inside His heart. Envisioning you, He said, "I long for you, I desire to pour out my deep love, kindness and goodness upon you."

God deeply desired children, yet before man was ever created God knew we were going to blow it. He wasn't caught off guard though – He is the all-knowing One. As a result of knowing ahead of time about our sinful failures, before He even created us He initiated a plan to rescue our lives from the power of sin. This act is called "redemption" in the Bible. He actually took care of the problem for us before we had even acted out the problem (The Lamb was slain before the foundation of the world – Revelation 13:8). God has never been caught off guard by mankind's failures – and that includes yours!

Years ago, I said to the Lord, "I wouldn't choose to have children if I knew ahead of time they were going to rebel, betray and dishonor me. I would be much happier without that type of child! Why then did You create us?" He spoke this clear word to me:

> My plan was to prove to mankind that My love would withstand every resistance. I allowed My love to be tested so that you would know it would always stand and never be withdrawn. I am Love.

> When anyone chooses to come into relationship with Me, they will never ever need to doubt My love for them. Knowing I passed every test, they will feel completely secure – and that is My desire.

That's how much He loves you. Isn't that amazing? Behold, what manner of love is this?

THE CROSS AND THE COVENANT

God's plan for you is to have an eternal relationship with Him that is established through a covenant. A covenant is a legally binding agreement between two people or parties. In order for a covenant to work, there needs to be absolute integrity in the making and the keeping of all its terms. Entering a covenant with a person of integrity gives you a sense of protection, a sense of security.

That's what the marriage covenant is supposed to be like. When you vow to be faithful to one another, to care for one another and honor each other, you should feel a sense of belonging and oneness with your covenant partner. That is the purpose of covenant. It legally secures relationship.

Mankind does not have a history of being good covenant keepers, so the very thing that should offer security is making many feel insecure. Some don't even bother getting married anymore because they think it might last or it might not. That is one reason why there is so much breakdown in the family these days. There are broken covenants everywhere and this is evidenced by the high divorce rate in our nation. God, however, is a covenant-keeping God. He is full of integrity and always keeps the terms of the covenants He makes.

The original use of the word covenant was, "where the blood flows." Ancient covenants always set terms, exchanged names, weapons, and resources. These covenants almost always included the consummation of the covenant through the mingling of blood. A covenant meal was served at the end of the ceremony and a celebration of this union commenced.

The marriage covenant is a blood covenant much like this. We make our vows before witnesses (which is an exchanging of terms), we exchange names (the bride usually takes her husband's name), and we exchange our resources (the assets of one legally become the other's in most cases). The marriage is then consummated through the sexual act, which breaks the hymen membrane (the shedding of blood). God's covenant plan for His relationship with man was a blood covenant (Christ's blood shed for us at the Cross). He set the terms, (through the Old Testament law and prophets) and then defined a name exchange (Jesus said, "In my name ask..."), a weapons exchange (Jesus' weapons and armor are ours), and a resource exchange (all our needs are met through Him).

In ancient civilizations, a representative of one tribe would cut covenant with a representative of another tribe. When the two leaders cut covenant on behalf of their people, then their entire tribe enjoyed the benefits of the covenant. This is what Christ did for us when He represented mankind in a covenant with God. Jesus Christ was and is our covenant representative and leader. It is His responsibility, as our covenant representative, to keep all the terms for us. In exchange, we receive all the covenant blessings. Wow!

3

The Amazing Good News

What I'm about to share with you is amazing. God desired to make a covenant with man that would secure us in relationship with Him for all eternity. However, He knew that once mankind fell, we would never keep a covenant. It was impossible because man became filled with a sin nature. To fulfill the covenant terms, God required a sinless representative for man who would keep all the conditions, but there was not a sinless person to be found. As a result, He chose to fill this position Himself. He chose to take our place in covenant by becoming a man. Jesus also took God's place in covenant because He is God. He is both Man and God. In reality then, He was cutting covenant with Himself. This is how God could cut an eternal, unbreakable, unfailing covenant with man. Jesus, who was fully God, left heaven and came into the sinful world as a man in order to fulfill this plan.

Many Christians don't understand this so I pray the light will go on for you today, because this truth is glorious. When you understand, you will worship and serve Him in full abandonment for all He has done. God loves you so much. He desires relationship with you even more than you desire relationship with Him. He knew you couldn't keep a covenant so He determined to become man and fulfill both sides of the covenant Himself. Jesus, the Son of God and Son of Man, made a covenant to include you in eternal relationship because you couldn't do it.

When He came as a man, He had to fulfill all of man's covenant terms which were laid out in Old Testament law. If He failed to fulfill every point of the law or if He gave in to temptation just once, He would not qualify to keep the covenant on man's behalf. This would have been devastating for us, but there was an even greater risk for Him. Jesus is referred to in Scripture as the last Adam. The first Adam was a perfect man before the fall. He was made in God's image and likeness. When he fell into temptation, the rule and dominion that had been given to him was surrendered over to Satan. Romans 6:16 teaches that when we submit ourselves to sin, we become sin's slave. This is what happened to Adam when he submitted to Satan's temptation, and this is what would have happened to the last Adam (Jesus), too, if He fell into even the slightest temptation. Only pure Love would be willing to take a risk like that.

JESUS THE MAN

Jesus came just like the first Adam. He was of man's nature yet without sin. He was to fulfill man's requirement in covenant with man's power, with man's capabilities. The Holy Spirit came upon Him to empower Him, just like the Holy Spirit empowers you today. Through the power of the Holy Spirit the man, Jesus, remained sinless throughout His entire life on the earth. You need to understand that He resisted sin in man's strength, with the power of the Holy Spirit helping Him. You'd better believe that there was a huge wrestle in His soul against sin, even though He was perfect and without sin in His nature. He had to wrestle just like the first Adam, because He had to secure the victory as a man in order to restore mankind to his rightful place in relationship with God. Ultimately Jesus Christ, at the end of His "covenant course," would be acknowledged not only as a perfect God but also as a perfect Man who would sit on a throne at the right hand of God. All things in heaven and in earth would ultimately be summed up in Him.

It was not easy for Christ to resist sin. In fact, at one point it was so grueling that He sweat drops of blood in His resistance against the temptations (Hebrews 12:4). He did it in man's power for you so you wouldn't have to do it, because you couldn't do it. Everything required for mankind to enter covenant with God was fulfilled through the man Jesus Christ. Jesus fulfilled all the law and the prophets.

JESUS COUNTS THE COST

Before the foundation of the world, Jesus probably had to ask Himself, "How big is My love? Am I willing to perform acts of love, kindness and mercy for people who don't even desire Me? Am I able to love so deeply that I would actually become sin for those whom I love? Am I willing to taste death for them?" He counted the cost and made a love choice with you in mind, saying, "Oh, yes! You are worth everything to Me. I will gladly leave heaven and pay the price, with joy!"

JESUS ARRIVES ON EARTH

Mary, a young virgin, conceived Jesus by the power of the Holy Spirit. She and Joseph traveled to Bethlehem, where Mary went into labor. There was no available lodging so Mary gave birth in an animal's stable and laid baby Jesus in a feeding trough. What kind of treatment was this for man's Savior? No palace, no special treatment and hardly anyone even discerned who He was.

He had to start passing love tests right away. If He had been offendable He could have thought: *Well, that's it, I'm going back to heaven. I tried to do something nice for you but you treated Me like an animal and threw Me in a feeding trough.* Jesus, however, did not take offense. In tremendous humility, He passed the love test. Even though He was worthy of the most extravagant treatment, He didn't demand it or expect it. He came to serve.

Herod even tried to have Him killed as a baby, but Jesus never stopped loving. He never withdrew love and never lost faith. What would you do if your only motivation was to help people and all of a sudden they're trying to kill you? You'd probably say something like, "I don't need you. I'll go somewhere else." But Jesus had a different heart.

HIS MINISTRY BEGINS

His childhood passed and His ministry began. He taught in the synagogues as a rabbi. The religious leaders examined His teachings carefully. They knew the Scriptures and were considered experts in the Word of God and doctrine. Jesus, however, is true doctrine. He is the living Word. He is true theology and yet He was called a blasphemer and a heretic by these very leaders. They attempted to bring legal charges against Him. This is the way they treated the true God.

How would you feel if you were God? There you are, teaching truth right from heaven. You're speaking truth because you *are* truth, and the people you came to save are saying, "You're a liar. You're a deceiver. You're a heretic.

You're teaching us false doctrine. You're demonized." Character assaults like this are much worse than simply saying, "Your theology is off."

I've experienced a little of that resistance myself and I must say those times were brutal. Everything in me wanted to withdraw. Jesus, however, never withdrew love from us, not for a moment. Each time He was opposed or mistreated by man, His love once again passed the test. He said, "I will never withdraw love and I will never stop believing in what can happen in your life." He kept consistent in faith and love through all the mistreatment.

Jesus chose twelve disciples and then seventy-two. He poured His time and life into them by giving, teaching, and mentoring day in and day out. Many others also followed His ministry. His own didn't always treat Him well, but even with all the disappointments He suffered, He never wavered in His commitment to them.

4

Love's Greatest Tests

The Garden of Gethsemane

One of Christ's most excruciating struggles was in Gethsemane (Gethsemane means "the oil press"). He faced every temptation that man would ever encounter. Strong forces of hell were spiritually assaulting Him. As we established earlier, Jesus had to resist sin as a man – in the same strength as the first Adam. You were in His heart the entire time He was wrestling against temptation. The pressure was so great against His soul that He sweat blood in His resistance against sin. With every drop of blood that pushed through His bursting capillaries He was saying, "For you, I will resist. No matter what it feels like. No matter how excruciating it is. My emotions are being rung out beyond explanation, but it's all for you. It's all for you."

I've faced some grueling spiritual battles and have engaged in warfare with powerful demonic entities. Although these seasons were unbearably painful, they were nothing at all in comparison to what Jesus experienced. I am a little aware, however, of the crushing feeling that pressures your emotions and your mind during such times. In the midst of this type of battle, it is essential to keep focused because all you have is the Word of God to stand on. Everything else that is going on in your life seems contrary to the truth and there's just one point of choice: "I will stand on Your Word, Lord, no matter what. I will trust my soul into Your keeping." It is all you have. At the end of these battles, your emotions, your thinking processes and even your physical body is weakened, fatigued and fragile. At times during these intense battles, I had to draw strength from God to even breathe. The impact of such warfare is very excruciating; I can't even find words to describe it. What I experienced, however, is still nothing in comparison to the pressure that Jesus experienced.

What was it like for Jesus when He had the hordes of hell trying to take Him out? What motivated Him to stand through this agony? God didn't *need* to put Himself in this position. Do you know why He did? It was His love for you. He said, "I'm doing this to fulfill your covenant requirements." He loves you that much. Just for a moment, forget about everyone else on the face of the earth. If you alone were left, He'd do it all over again. In the midst of Gethsemane's agony, you were in His vision. The thought of having you with Him for all eternity was His motivation to continue. Your face gave Him the strength to endure.

BETRAYED BY A FRIEND

When Jesus departed from the garden He was weak and exhausted. Judas, one of His twelve disciples, approached Him, betraying Him with a kiss. Even though Jesus knew Judas would betray Him, He continued to call him friend. He said, "Friend, do what you have come for" (Matthew 26:50). Betrayal is very painful. If you have been betrayed, you know how difficult this is on your emotions, but even betrayal could not make Jesus withdraw love or friendship. There is nothing you can do to make Him withdraw His love. You can treat God terribly. You can tell Him to leave you alone, but He will never withdraw love from you. He'll continue to say, "I love you."

ABANDONED AND DENIED

I can't imagine what it would feel like to be in a ferocious spiritual battle and then experience betrayal by a close friend and co-worker. To top it all off, though, all His followers fled when He was arrested. When you're in a hard place, being falsely accused, you just want someone, even if it's only one, to stand with you. *Is there one that will just come to My side right now? Is there one who will believe in Me? Is there one who will defend Me?* Jesus did not even have one. His own disciples, whom He had poured into for three years, all fled in fear of their reputation.

As Jesus was led away He heard Peter, one of His closest disciples, swearing, "No, I never knew Him." Oh how painful it must have been for Jesus when He heard that denial. He knew prophetically that Peter would do this, but foreknowledge doesn't ease the emotional devastation when it actually happens.

> Peter, I need you right now. Are you so afraid for your own life that you wouldn't even admit you know Me? Peter, look into My eyes and see My pain. See My love. You have denied Me but You cannot make Me withdraw love from you.

HIS TRIAL

False witnesses were paid to testify against Jesus in court. That is harsh! When you know someone is lying about you, the natural tendency is to immediately defend yourself. Isaiah 53:7 reveals, though, that Jesus was like a lamb led to the slaughter, silent before His shearers, not opening His mouth in His own defense. He had purposed in His heart to offer unconditional love and mercy toward the lying witnesses.

You can line your pockets with filthy
lucre, but you cannot make Me withdraw
My love from you.

They stripped Him naked, placed a crown of thorns
on His head and mocked Him openly. Even though you
and I were not yet created, we were there, hidden in the
heart of depraved humanity. We might think that we
would never hurt or deny Him, but like Peter we might
not understand the weakness of our own flesh. It is probable that each of us would have done the same thing.

Christ's love was being severely tested by mankind.
You and I have put His love to the test many times and
yet He has never abandoned us and neither has He withdrawn love. He never will.

Beaten and Scourged

Jesus was beaten, spit upon and mocked. His face
was violently struck, apparently making Him unrecognizable. Again, with every cruel punch, His response was
only love as He gazed into the eyes of His afflicters.

He was brutally scourged with a whip that had nine
leather strips. At the end of each strip were little pieces
of sharp metal or bone. Each stroke provided nine lashings. It was a common belief that 40 lashes would bring
death. Under Roman laws He might have received even
more. History reveals that His flesh was literally ripped
open and that His innards were exposed. Every time the

razor-sharp edge of the whip dug into His flesh, you were in His heart. Your face was constantly before Him. You were the reason He could endure such hostility. Looking into the face of those who were cruelly scourging Him, He would have said once again, "You cannot make Me withdraw My love." He would have assured you, too, if it was your hand holding the scourge.

CRUCIFIED

Jesus carried the heavy wooden cross that was heaved onto His back. Weakened with pain, He staggered up to Calvary's hill. An angry mob followed Him, mocking, ridiculing and shouting, "Crucify Him, crucify Him." They nailed His hands and feet to the cross and hung Him between two guilty criminals. They were crucifying an innocent man.

To many, it looked like Jesus' life was being taken. It appeared that Jesus was defeated, but His life wasn't taken – *it was given!* The devil did not take Jesus' life. The false witnesses did not take His life. The Jews did not kill Him. The Romans did not kill Him. You did not kill Him. No one killed Him. He freely gave His life. When you see Jesus hanging on the cross, you see Love Himself hanging there – a free gift of love – love that had been completely proven and tested against everything that could possibly oppose or destroy it.

Love Himself was on that cross, stripped naked and humiliated, hanging there in agonizing pain. In the midst of this agony, one of the thieves asked to be saved. Jesus didn't hesitate. In His greatest point of need, He continued to pour Himself out. He could have said, "What do you mean, you want a favor from Me? Really? I don't deserve to be here and you do. Forget it, it's too late!" Jesus wasn't and isn't like that. He proved His love once again, "Of course, I will save you. In fact, today I'll do it and you will be with Me in paradise. You will see the glory of My salvation."

Looking down from His cross, Jesus saw a mass of people – a crowd who delighted to watch Him die. "If You're the Son of God, come down off that cross and save Yourself." His merciful, loving retaliation was, "Father, forgive them; for they do not know what they are doing" (Luke 23:34).

Can you imagine? We sometimes find it difficult to forgive those who hurt or offend us. Consider Jesus: a mass of angry people rallied against Him, and you were there, too – all humanity was. Oh yes, He saw your face in the crowd that day. We all sinned against Him and yet He said, "Father, forgive them all." He forgave all the sins of mankind right at that point. He cancelled the debt of sin. Only pure Love Himself can do that.

He went even further and actually became mankind's sin. Jesus chose to become sin. He chose to have your sin poured into Him so that He could pour His righteousness into you. He chose to become something abhorrent that would be judged so you would be free from judgment.

Have you ever been mistreated, taken advantage of or sinned against? Doesn't it give you a great feeling to see the offender punished, knowing they're getting what they deserve? But Jesus' heart was different. He said, "No, I'll take the punishment for your sin. I'll take full responsibility. You can go free."

A number of years ago I was on the mission field. I misjudged a particular situation and consequently made some bad decisions. My actions seriously hurt some individuals. When I finally saw the situation clearly I was terribly grieved, overwhelmed, and deeply ashamed. I thought: I should have known better, I shouldn't have done that. It was difficult for me to believe that I hadn't seen the situation through eyes of wisdom in the first place. I asked for forgiveness from one individual who was particularly wounded through the process. They refused to extend the undeserved mercy that I desperately needed. For years afterward, I had a very difficult time forgiving myself.

One day, I was crying out to the Lord in prayer, "Don't let my failure continue to hurt them. Don't let it ruin their lives." I felt terrible to the very core of my being.

The Lord spoke very soberly to me, "You didn't commit that sin. You didn't make that mistake. I did."

"What? No, Lord! You never did that. I'm the one who did it."

"I did it," He insisted.

"Jesus, no You didn't. You are perfect and You have never wronged anyone, ever!"

He tenderly responded, "I bore your mistake on the Cross 2,000 years ago. I chose to take full responsibility for this mistake so that you might go free. I have even borne the judgment for it. You are free! I became this sin for you and in exchange I have given you My righteousness. This has all been paid in full. If there is any further problem, that hurting individual will need to come to Me. You have been totally released and fully justified. You never did it!"

I burst into tears, tears of gratitude that flowed from deep inside my being. How can I not love a God who showed that much mercy? He clearly revealed to me that day that this is what He's done for us all. This is what is called "substitution." He literally took our judgment and in exchange, gave us His life and righteousness. Oh my, can we fully grasp this?

5

FOR ALL PEOPLE AND FOR ALL TIME

God's love for us today is no different than it was for the sinful crowd at the foot of the cross 2,000 years ago. He performed an eternal exchange, saying, "It is no longer you that sinned, but Me. I have become your sin. I have paid the penalty. I have taken full responsibility. It is no longer your issue." Love laid down His life for all people. Love laid down His life for you! You are free!

DYING IN FAITH

Gazing at you through the portals of time, Jesus died on the cross in love and in faith. He gave up the ghost and cried out, "It is finished." Helpless, but remaining in faith, He entrusted His life into the hands of His Father. When He became your sin, He had no power to raise

Himself from the dead. God planned Christ's resurrection before the foundation of the world. And Jesus believed Him.

After His death, Jesus descended into the lower parts of the earth. On the third day, His heavenly Father raised Him from the dead. Mary and the other women, the disciples and many others literally saw Him walking the earth following His resurrection. Oh yes, He is the Resurrection and the Life – the First Born from the dead! When He was raised from the dead, He took the keys of death and of hell. He stripped the devil of his authority and made an open show of him. Oh, what an eternal victory!

JESUS CHRIST IS FOREVER

THE RESURRECTION AND THE LIFE

Jesus has invited everyone into eternal relationship with God through simply receiving Him as Savior by faith. All the work for mankind's redemption has been completed in Christ – finished! He did it all for us. The only thing left for us to do is to simply believe. Mankind's identity is found in Jesus – the One who accomplished everything for us. No man can boast in his own ability to save himself. Jesus fully paid the debt that we could not pay. He fully accomplished the work that we could not do. All glory to Him!

Jesus walked the earth for forty days after His resurrection from the dead and then gloriously ascended to heaven. He is forever seated at the right hand of God, far above all principalities, powers, and every name that is named (Ephesians 1:20-22). We are seated with Jesus in the heavenly places when we receive Him as our Savior (Ephesians 2:6). Our life is hidden with God in Christ (Colossians 3:3).

SEALED IN THE COVENANT

Everyone who believes in Christ has the gift of everlasting life – His abundant life. Everyone who believes in Him is forever sealed into covenant, a legally binding love agreement between God and man. This covenant is an eternal covenant. It is impossible for it to be broken because it is between Jesus, Man and Jesus, God. Jesus won our place for us through His own sinless life. When you believe in Him, you are saved from the separation from God that sin creates. Your identity as a Kingdom child is not in your own ability to accomplish anything. It is in His completed work – His ability – past tense. It is done! It is finished!

In fact, if we were to be absolutely honest right now, you are an utter failure outside of Christ. It is impossible for you to please God in your own strength – absolutely impossible! The only way anyone can please God is by believing in Christ. The arms of Jesus are open to all sinners. If you receive Jesus as Savior, then your identity is in Him. You are in Christ, a brand new creation. You are eternally one with Him. It is simple faith that connects you to this glorious eternal salvation. That's all you have to do – simply believe. That's it. That's all. Ephesians 2:8-9, says "For by grace you have been saved through faith; and that not of yourselves, it is the gift of God; not as a result of works, that no one may boast."

What is this grace that saves us? It is His divine influence in your life. It is His choice to accomplish everything for you. It is His work of favor over you – undeserved favor. You don't deserve it, I don't deserve it. No one does. It's undeserved, unmerited favor. It's His influence that comes upon your heart. You have been saved by grace through faith. Simple faith is what connects you to the glorious, finished work of the Cross. When you make this "faith connection," you become a brand new creation. Second Corinthians 5:17 states, "Therefore, if anyone *is* in Christ, *he is* a new creation; old things have passed away; behold, all things have become new" (NKJV).

Ah, what a glorious life we have been given in Christ – a brand new life, an eternal relationship with God Himself. Christ did all this for YOU! You see how precious you are? God loves you with an everlasting love ... He really does!

Perhaps you have just read this through and your heart is longing to become God's child. It's simple. The following is a little prayer. If it represents your desire, why don't you go ahead and pray it from your heart. God will hear you. His gift of life and love will enter you, and your journey begins!

DEAR HEAVENLY FATHER,

Thank You for loving me so perfectly through Your Son, Jesus Christ, and for offering me eternal life through the finished work of the Cross. I turn away from a self-ruled life and invite Jesus Christ to enter my heart as my personal Savior and Lord.

Come into my life, Lord Jesus, and forgive me of all my sin. Give me new life within and make me the person You want me to be. I believe that You are now in my heart and my new life has begun. I now belong to You. You are my God. Thank You, Father. AMEN

YOUR NEW LIFE BEGINS

When you receive Jesus as your personal Savior by faith, His life enters your spirit. You are now what the Scripture calls *born again* (Read John 3:1-9). You have Christ's brand new life inside you. His purity, love, peace, truth and blessings are now inside your spirit. You are so beautiful and perfect within.

Just like a new baby, in the natural, needs nourishment and care, so do new babies in the Lord. The Bible is full of truth that is like fresh milk and food for you. As you read it each day, it will nourish you and reveal wonderful things about God's love and His ways. You will also want to meet some other Christians who understand the love of God. Fellowshipping with other followers of Jesus is so much fun. Take some time and visit some churches in your area. Christ's Holy Spirit dwells within you and He will direct you to a good fellowship if you ask Him to.

As a child of your heavenly Father, you are invited to communicate with Him through prayer. Prayer is easy – you simply share your heart with Him. He loves to answer your desires. Some good teachings on prayer will help you to grow in the many different ways that you can communicate with God. Prayer is very fulfilling and powerful.

All of God's goodness belongs to you when you are in Christ ... so imbibe of it all. You have been called to a full and glorious life in Jesus. Enjoy!

6

A DECREE

Proclaim this decree often over your life!

The Lord loves me with an everlasting love and has promised to give me a future and a hope. With loving-kindness, He has drawn me unto Himself. I look carefully and intently at the manner of love the Father has poured out upon me. It is through this love that He has called me to be His dear child. I am completely and fully accepted in Him, my God and Savior. Nothing can separate me from the love of God that is in Christ Jesus my Lord – not tribulation or distress, not persecution, famine or nakedness, not peril, sword, angels, principalities, powers, death, or life; neither things present nor things to come – absolutely nothing can separate me from the love of God which is in Christ Jesus my Lord.

God's love toward me is patient and kind. His love for me bears all things, believes all things, hopes all things and endures all things. His love will never fail. His love for me is so rich that He gave His only begotten Son. Because of this, I will never perish but have everlasting life with Him. As a result of God's great love for me, I have an unbreakable, eternal covenant with Him. Through this covenant of love, He has put His laws within my heart and written His commandments upon my mind.

I have been invited to the Lord's banqueting table, and His banner over me is love! His love is better than the choicest of wines. Through His intimate love, He draws me and invites me to follow after Him. I am fair and pleasant unto Him. I am rooted and grounded in His love, well able to comprehend with all believers the width and length and depth and height of His unfailing love. I have been called to know this rich love that surpasses knowledge so that I may be filled with all the fullness of God.

I truly am the object of God's

deepest love

and affection.

*Activate your God-given power
to create realms and atmospheres*

CREATE YOUR WORLD

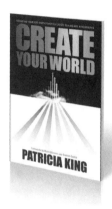

No one deliberately chooses a life of
failure and despair, a humdrum life going
nowhere, so why do so many people live
there? Discover twelve keys that will open
the gates of goodness into a realm of favor,
joy, pleasure and success... don't settle for
anything less than God's intent for your
life. He's given you the power to Create
Your World!

Decree the Word!
Third Edition

Decree a thing and it shall be established.
Job 22:28

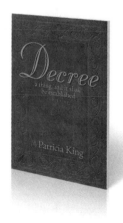

The Word of God is powerful and it will
profoundly influence your life. *Decree*
helps believers activate the power of the
Word in key areas of their lives, including
health, provision, love, wisdom, family,
business, spiritual strength, blessing, favor,
and prayer. The third edition includes four
new decrees: "Rejuvenation," "Greater
Grace," "12 Prayers for Your Nation," and
"I Am Supernatural in Christ."

PATRICIA KING

Patricia King is president of XP Ministries and co-founder of XPmedia.com, Inc. She has been a pioneering voice in ministry, with over 30 years of background as a Christian minister in conference speaking, prophetic service, church leadership, and television & radio appearances. Patricia has written numerous books, produced many CDs and DVDs, hosts the TV program "Patricia King-Everlasting Love," and is the CEO of a number of businesses. Patricia's reputation in the Christian community is world-renowned.

Christian Services Association (CSA) was founded in Canada in 1973 and in the USA in 1984. It is the parent ministry of XP Ministries, a 501-C3 founded in 2004 in Arizona. They are located in Maricopa, AZ and Kelowna, B.C. Patricia King and numerous team members equip the body of Christ in the gifts of the Spirit, prophetic ministry, intercession, and evangelism. XP Ministries/XPmedia is called to spreading the gospel through media.

AUTHOR CONTACT INFORMATION

U.S. Ministry Center
P.O. Box 1017
Maricopa, AZ 85139

Canada Ministry Center
3054 Springfield Road
Kelowna, B.C. VIX 1A5

E-mail: info@XPmedia.com

XPministries.com
XPmedia.com
XPmissions.com
PatriciaKing.com